Sam looks for the keeper.

He looks right into a big cat.

He sees the keeper asleep!

Sam rubs the big cat ...

... out comes the keeper!

Sam looks for the missing animals.

Freezer Phil

He spots Freezer Phil pinching them!

Sam and Siss go to Freezer Phil's den.

They spot all the missing animals.

Freezer Phil has been freezing their zoo!

Sam and Siss must get the Frost Zapper.

It is off to jail for Freezer Phil.

Oh! Jail is no fun!

Nee nar!

Nee nar!

Whizz!

Sam returns the animals to the zoo.
He thinks all is well, but …

Sam looks for the little ring.

The ring is in Siss!

Miss Plum will get the ring back soon.